MICHAEL DA[

ARE YOU GOING TO HEAVEN OR HELL

TRILOGY
A WHOLLY OWNED SUBSIDIARY OF **TBN**
PROFESSIONAL PUBLISHING MEETS POWERFUL PROMOTION

Trilogy Christian Publishers
A Wholly Owned Subsidiary of Trinity Broadcasting Network
2442 Michelle Drive
Tustin, CA 92780
Copyright © 2025 by Michael David Klijanowicz
All Scripture quotations, unless otherwise noted, taken from THE HOLY BIBLE, NEW INTERNATIONAL VERSION®, NIV® Copyright © 1973, 1978, 1984, 2011 by Biblica, Inc.® Used by permission. All rights reserved worldwide.
All rights reserved, including the right to reproduce this book or portions thereof in any form whatsoever.
For information, address Trilogy Christian Publishing
Rights Department, 2442 Michelle Drive, Tustin, CA 92780.
Trilogy Christian Publishing/ TBN and colophon are trademarks of Trinity Broadcasting Network.
For information about special discounts for bulk purchases, please contact Trilogy Christian Publishing.

Trilogy Disclaimer: The views and content expressed in this book are those of the author and may not necessarily reflect the views and doctrine of Trilogy Christian Publishing or the Trinity Broadcasting Network.

10 9 8 7 6 5 4 3 2 1
Library of Congress Cataloging-in-Publication Data is available.
ISBN 979-8-89597-206-9
ISBN 979-8-89597-207-6 (ebook)

ACKNOWLEDGEMENTS:

I would like to thank God for giving me the vision and wisdom to write this book. Without the help of the Spirit, there is no way this book would have been able to be written in two days (not including editing). I would like to thank my wife again for her continued love and support of me even through my darkest hours of my darkest days. I would also like to thank ALL of my different Bible brothers out there who are true warriors in Christ as well as all of the great people that have befriended me and accepted me at Celebrate Recovery—you all know who you are. And finally, I would like to acknowledge you, the reader of this book; this may just be the most important book that you have ever read in your entire life; once you are done reading it, either share your copy with someone else or tell someone else about it. This is the way we will spread these messages to everyone else around the world.

ABOUT THE AUTHOR

Michael David Klijanowicz is from Fallston, Maryland, and is married to his wife, and they have two kids together, a son and a daughter. He has worked hard his entire life through all different kinds of employment to get the success he has achieved so far in this life, but he almost lost it all through his own negative actions, following his own ego, pride, greed, and not including who the most important person should have been in his life: God. However, Mike eventually found God through a wild process, and it changed his entire life as well as his outlook on life. Mike has learned that life is not about things or what you have or how much money you make or have, but it is instead about how much you help others, especially those in significant need. We must all turn our lives over to God and completely surrender ourselves so we can take a journey with Jesus. It says this in the Bible, as you will see in this book, and it's how you can help your case on getting into heaven instead of going to hell when your time comes to meet the Creator. We are all going to die one day, and a decision will be made as to if we are going to be accepted into Heaven or sent to hell based on everything that we choose to do or not to do in this life that we got to live. Don't wait until it's too late. Don't give up because life is too hard or it seems impossible; Mike has been there too. It is never too late to turn your life around and surrender to God. The sooner you turn your life over to God and start living your life walking with Jesus every single day, the better and better your life will become, and you will be helping to plead your case in the end on why you deserve to go to Heaven. Mike is a great Believer in God and Jesus and the Holy Spirit, and he knows that there is a place in this world that feels like Heaven where almost all of your problems can be cured. To be able to truly live in a place and a world of absolute peace, joy, and happiness is not only possible but is very probable if you take up your cross and walk with Jesus every single day. There is a place you can get to in your life that is so beautiful and so peaceful, where you no longer experience stress, anxiety, worry, fear, depression, pain, and so many other mental and physical health disorders. All you have to do is just surrender yourself to God and let your ego and pride go and drift away. Mike truly hopes by writing this book that as many people out there get to experience what it truly feels like to be saved by God and to be reborn again as true believers in Christ. If you don't know how you can get there but want to get there, then this book is for you. Think of it as a self-help quick guide on how to completely transform your life spiritually: a book that you can read in one single sitting in a couple short hours of your time that is very easy to read and to follow. You will see there is A

LOT more that you need to do to prove to God that you are worthy of entering Heaven than just going to church, singing songs, and making a donation once a week and then going right back into the world living in sin the rest of the week. The biggest impact that Mike likes to think about that this book could have is changing the world one person at a time so they can start shining their light of Christ into this world of darkness for others to see so they will want to learn how to shine their light as well, until darkness is completely eradicated from the world and we can all live in complete peace, joy, and happiness. Mike knows that seems like an audacious goal, but with God, ANYTHING is possible, and He helped Mike write this book through the Spirit. It only took Mike two days to write this book, and there is no way he could have done that on his own when the largest paper he had ever written was only about ten pages in college. Mike truly hopes that anyone who picks this book up enjoys reading it as much as he did writing it. This book is not about Mike; instead, it is about you and your own salvation. This book is about getting you to really think about what the most important thing in this life really is and why. Now, let's begin your transformation and your journey with Jesus…

TABLE OF CONTENTS

Acknowledgements: 5

About The Author 7

Why Are We Here In the First Place? 15

Why Did I Decide to Write this Book? 21

Mike's Testimony and Background 25

So How Do You Start Your Journey with Jesus? 51

Now, Why is it Important to Do All this Stuff? 71

ARE YOU GOING TO HEAVEN OR HELL?

"Not everyone who says to me, Lord, Lord, will enter the kingdom of heaven, but only the one who does the will of my Father who is in heaven."

Matthew 7:21

WHY ARE WE HERE IN THE FIRST PLACE?

This is kind of a double-sided question because as you will see I have two answers to the question. The first answer is it all started one afternoon outside of one of my Bible study meetings in Churchville, MD. As we normally do, after our hour-long Bible study, a few of us hang around afterwards and discuss things in the parking lot, oftentimes for two+ hours after our group meeting. Well on a particular day, I decided to stay after with two of my fellow Bible brothers, and the discussion of Heaven and hell came up. One of my fellow comrades told us a story of his own daughter who had died in Nigeria (his home country). He told us a couple of days before her death she was sedated in the hospital and finally had a long night sleep and also had a very vivid spiritual dream. She called her father immediately the next morning and told him that she had a dream where she saw Heaven and got very scared during her dream. He asked her why she was scared, and she said, "Well, there was a very long line of people ahead of her, and each person would take their time to move forward to meet Jesus and an angel would be with them with a big book" (a book of the person's life also referred as the Lamb's Book of Life in Revelation 13:8). His daughter said that the majority of the people, almost ALL of the people, that were in front of her in line were all sent to hell and not let into Heaven, and she was very nervous to meet Jesus because she thought that she was going to be sent to hell as well. Well, it turns out she was saved by God, and the angel moved her into Heaven, but she couldn't believe that almost everyone who went before her got sent into hell. This got us all to talking and discussing that the majority (we estimated probably close to 95%) of people on earth have not been saved by God and do not live their lives of the Spirit; instead, they live their lives of the flesh and world in sin. I immediately thought of people I know who are close to me and who I wanted to be saved ASAP, but I realized that everyone has to do their own spiritual journey with Jesus. So I thought, "Well, then I will do a podcast about it, and surely people will listen to that, and it will change their lives. Sadly, the podcast got fewer than ten views, so I prayed about it, and eventually with God's help, I decided I needed to write a book about this topic along with sharing my own story on how I was personally saved by God, and that is how we are here.

Secondly, let's start with this question and go from there. Why are we, humans, here on this earth? What is the point of our existence? Were we created to live the way 95% of us do now—grow up, graduate high school or college or some advanced educational institution to get a job that we work at until we are seventy to seventy-five years old only to retire and spend the rest of our lives in diapers until we die ten years later (feeling like our lives were unhappy and unfulfilled)? I am going to go out on a limb and say that I doubt the Creator of ALL of us had this in mind as to how He wanted us to live out our lives.

Instead, I would argue that we are here, born here on this planet, to complete an "audition." This is the audition of a lifetime where every single thing you do is recorded and captured to be analyzed at the end of your life by God to determine if you are in fact worthy enough to enter into His Kingdom of Heaven or if you will wind up in hell instead, due to the conscious AND unconscious CHOICES that you made throughout your life. When I think of every single thing you do and every choice you make, I think about the song by The Police called "Every Breath You Take." Basically, it says that no matter what you do, "I'll be watching you." When I hear this song, I think about God watching every breath you take and always being there watching EVERYTHING you do.

God is watching EVERYTHING we do ALL the time, AND it is ALL getting recorded and written down in your very own book of life, which will be opened when you wait your turn in line to meet with Jesus after you die. What He wants to see is a FAITHFUL and OBEDIENT servant who followed his commandments and lived a life of Faith and Trust with Jesus serving as your example of how to model your life. After all, that is why Jesus was sent to Earth in the first place, to teach ALL of us How to live the RIGHT WAY. How to live His Way! And instead of people embracing Him and His teachings, they mocked Him and killed Him (only because He allowed them to do this for a MUCH BIGGER purpose).

Now, WHY are we ALL here? I am going to go out on a limb and say, knowing God, it is for some HUGE PURPOSE! For a MUCH HIGHER purpose than most of us can even fathom. I believe we are ALL here not only to EARN our way into Heaven but to transform this world that we live in, one person at a time. You see, each of us has a light inside of us, call it a spirit if you want, that we emulate out to the world. The larger our connection to God, the larger our light/spirit gets and the more we can use our light/spirit to help grow the Kingdom of God, which is exactly what my hopes are with writing this book. And I can assure you that as I am typing this on my computer using my old version of Microsoft Word 2007 (even though its 2024—hey, if it ain't broke, don't fix it), the Holy Spirit is right here with me and is helping my fingers move to put the exact right words down at the exact right places on this paper, which will hopefully become a book, that every single person in the world reads and uses it to TRANSFORM THEIR LIVES. In fact, without the Holy Spirit's help, it would have been absolutely IMPOSSIBLE for me to write this entire book in just two days. The wisdom and knowledge contained inside of this book was given to me directly by God through various ways that He chooses to communicate with me (social media videos, music/songs, tv shows/movies, books, radio stations, podcasts, etc.). To give you an example of this and how He communicates with me through music, two of my most favorite songs with God are 1) "Nothing's Gonna Stop Us Now" by Starship and 2) "Another Day in Paradise" by Phil Collins. The reason these are my favorite songs from God are because He would make them show up in my Facebook reels feed over and over again, trying to almost send me a message that I needed to decipher with them. Now, some may say it is just the algorithm showing me the song videos over and over again, but I do not feel that way. When I get shown the "Nothing's Gonna Stop Us Now" song, it is usually after I just learned about a new idea from God, and the song's lyrics are saying that NOTHING is gonna stop US (Me and God) with what we are doing together to encourage me to keep moving forward on the idea. I usually see the "Another Day in Paradise" song come on when I am on my way somewhere in my car, and it is a reminder to me from God that we are living in Another Day in Paradise in complete absolute peace, joy, and happiness (even though we are in the real world) together, and I will soon be called to help someone with something.

At this point, it is also important to understand that we live in two worlds here on earth: the world of the flesh and the world of the Spirit. In the world of the Spirit, we cannot see anything, but this is where both Good and evil spirits communicate with us. Hollywood doesn't always tell the truth, or at least the whole truth, but they do have the Good vs. evil thing right. Right now in this world, there is a very serious and true spiritual war going on between Good and evil, or how I like to think of it is between the Light and darkness. My goal in this book will be to provide you with actual scriptures from the Bible to backup or justify what I am saying or claiming in certain parts of the book so you know I am not just simply making stuff up out of thin air.

WHY DID I DECIDE TO WRITE THIS BOOK?

The simple answer to this question is basically the same reason I started my YouTube podcast called, "Is Jesus Real?" (It's easiest to find if you Google "Klijanowicz YouTube"), and that is to bring as many people to Christ as I possibly can. I have been called by God to use my creativity (with His help, wisdom, and knowledge) to help the Kingdom accomplish some of its goals, by bringing as many people as I can back to the Faith (which may be just a part of the overall larger goal that I will talk about later on in the book). Some may already be with the Faith AND Spirit AND living their lives in the Spirit; some may believe in God and Jesus and the Spirit and go to church to worship and are genuinely good people (is that enough to get into Heaven?); some may kind of believe in a greater power out there but aren't convinced there is a God. Bottom line is: I wanted to write a book that could be for EVERYONE, no matter how far along on your own personal faith journey you are. I have also noticed that a MAJORITY of people in the world live their own lives according to themselves, and they make their own decisions based off of their own desires of the flesh that they have, instead of making decisions based on what God wants for them or what God thinks is the best option for them. Most of the time, that is because God is absent from their lives due to their own choices.

My goal is to write a brief book that is easy to read in one sitting in good old plain English, which also helps people understand how and why the Bible is so important to us, even though many find it very hard to read and to comprehend. That all being said, "my way" (also known as Mike's way) is NOT the "only way" to be saved, get born again, and to develop an extremely deep relationship with God. Every single person on this earth will have to take their own unique spiritual walk, spiritual journey, or as I like to call it, spiritual ADVENTURE with Jesus and the Holy Spirit leading the way.

I also want this book to be extremely authentic, one that the average person can easily relate to. I will be talking about some extremely uncomfortable issues, including suicide, and want to warn you now so you are not surprised when it appears. Remember, EVERYTHING in this book, just like EVERYTHING in life, is designed to make you STRONGER. When you go through adversity in your own life, it is God's way of teaching you how to be a stronger person, even though that is the absolute last thing you will

WHY DID I DECIDE TO WRITE THIS BOOK?

think about when going through it.

I also want to make a promise to you: that you can live a life full of nothing but Absolute True PEACE, JOY, and HAPPINESS from start to finish EVERY SINGLE DAY of your life AND eliminate all worry, stress, anxiety, pain, depression, other mental and physical health problems, etc. All you have to do is TRUST ME, follow my instructions, and TAKE THIS BOOK SERIOUSLY! You see, this is just another benefit that God gives you if you do your walk the right way, do what he asks of you, and show Him obedience and loyalty. You will not only ensure that you get access into the party of your life for ETERNITY in Heaven, you will literally be able to live in Heaven on Earth down here on this planet while you are waiting for your turn to meet Jesus. Think about death like that; there is absolutely no need to be worried or scared or anxious about death. Instead, think about it like this: It is your time when you get to meet Jesus. How great is that! I personally can't wait until that day comes, but in the meantime, I will live my life to the fullest, serve God in EVERY SINGLE WAY that I can and serve my fellow man and woman as well.

In this next section of the book, I am going to go over exactly what happened with me. You will see how I got so connected to God so fast. It is a very WILD story. This is what I always thought I was going to be writing my book about: my story, my testimony of how God helped me and changed my life. I never thought I would be writing an entire different story about Heaven and hell to help as many people as I can in this entire world get into Heaven and help to truly make this world a better place, but this book is God's will, not mine. You see, when you look at the implications that this book could have if everyone on the planet read it, it could flat out change the world and ELMINATE all of the evil in it. Imagine a world with no wars, no greedy corporations that could care less about people's overall health (food companies, insurance companies, drug companies, etc.), people who truly care about helping others in this world (instead of just making a profit for their shareholders), who are in need of the basics like running water, electric, etc.. I mean, this world could completely be transformed and could actually become Heaven on earth for EVERYONE, IF enough other people actually change their lives and behaviors and BELIEFS...

MIKE'S TESTIMONY AND BACKGROUND

I was born into a family with a mother and father and eventually had a little brother in Parkville, MD. I grew up there most of my life in a highly dysfunctional home where I was emotionally abused for most of my young life. This led me to "acting out" as a child and eventually a young adult as well. I got drunk for the first time in fifth grade, was smoking cigarettes and hanging out at the roller skating rink and pool hall by age of twelve, and started abusing marijuana "recreationally" around fourteen or so. This is really when we finally started going to church as a family, when I was in drug recovery. I didn't get much out of it; sometimes what the priest said made some sense to me, but that was about it. I was able to pretty much turn my life around by the end of my high school years, but I was still voted and known as the party animal of my senior class. I will admit it was a lot of fun living that way, and I never thought it would ever catch up to me until I was failing all of my classes. What I was really doing was medicating myself from my problems that I faced at home. My dad was never there; he was always at work where he went at 4:00am and didn't get home until 7:30pm (he worked in D.C. about 1.5 hours from our house), so everything was up to my mom. She smoked cigarettes and drank wine just about every night from her wine box in the fridge, but she had a lot to deal with. And even though she drank pretty much every night from what I can remember, I never thought she was an alcoholic because to me she was just my mom. She had me and my brother, who also had a lot of his own learning problems and had to take medications for that, which also gave him really bad acne and sores all over his body. He also developed a nervous tick, which I was convinced was from all of the emotional abuse that we suffered in that home. Eventually his sores healed up, and he "grew out" of his nervous tick.

Once I turned fourteen years old, I decided I was going to get a job, and that is exactly what I got. I have always had a job since I have been fourteen years old. My first job was a busboy in a restaurant of a trashy hotel not far from my high school. I have worked in fast food, a meat market butcher shop, roller skating rink, higher end restaurants, and everyday restaurants. I have done just about all the jobs from mopping the floors, washing dishes, to bussing tables, to waiting tables, to being the bar back, to being a bartender

MIKE'S TESTIMONY AND BACKGROUND

and even a bouncer at the front door, checking ID's and taking cover charges. I eventually went to community college and got all of my general education requirements/credits out of the way in about two years and transferred to Towson University where I was lucky enough to be able to live on campus because I didn't want to live in my home, and I honestly don't think my parents wanted me living there either. I went through my two years at Towson and halfway through my junior year met my present wife.

I could write a book about how we met, but long story short, I actually met her sister first as she was in classes with me when I was in community college. We stayed in touch on our pagers and landlines because we didn't have cell phones yet. About a year or so after I met my wife at community college through her sister, she called me and asked me to go to a bull roast with her and her parents; they had an extra ticket, so I went, and the rest was history.

Once I graduated college, all I wanted to do was to become a police officer so I could work with the public and help people. I mean, I was obsessed with becoming a police officer; I had all the police quest games and had been playing them on our home computer since I was young. The only problem was that I did still smoke cigarettes and was a little out of shape as far as the physical "running" test went because I was a "bigger" guy. I trained and trained and had no issues with the bench press or sit ups or anything else, except the darn run. I could never get the time down. You had to do 1.5 miles in 11 minutes and 51 seconds. No matter what I did, I just couldn't do it, it's not easy when you are 6'0" and 265lbs. Anyway, I went ahead and started the application process, and it was to take the written exam and the physical exam on the same day. The problem was, I dropped a keg of beer on my leg at work as a bar back that gave me a huge bruise, so I couldn't run. They postponed me and let me do the physical examinations with the people that failed theirs the first time they took it, which was a few weeks later. So I loaded up on about five or six ripped fuel tablets (basically all caffeine) and went to the physical exam. Right before the physical exam started, they put a piece of paper in front of me, and it had, like, four or five questions on it, one of which was, "Have you ever done any drugs, and if so, what and how much and how often." At this moment in my life, I was faced with a choice: Do I not tell the truth and get into the police department if I pass the physical tests (although I would also need to take a polygraph too), or do I tell the truth and pretty much know I was not gonna make it. Well, I decided to tell the truth, even though A LOT of my other friends who used to buy drugs from me went on to become police officers, and a few are still police officers to this day. The silver lining was I actually did pass all of the physical tests, including the run, but it wasn't until the next day that I found out that they were not going to be accepting me. The ironic part about this is that now, 25+ years later, they would accept me even with the drug history that I had when I did them as a young adult, as their standards have changed throughout the years as drug use becomes increasingly more acceptable in our society (which is crazy to me).

So now that my entire life's dream was basically gone because I told the truth and "did the right thing," I had to figure out something else to do with my time to make money so I could MOVE OUT of my parents' house ASAP! I got a job as a substance abuse counselor at a local juvenile detention facility and had absolutely ZERO on-the-job-training or help at all. They just threw me to the "wolves" or the juvenile "inmates" at the facility. It didn't take long for me to realize that was not the job for me. I saw an ad in the paper for another position that opened for a juvenile probation officer, but you had to take a written examination and have a four-year degree. I had the degree, so I just had to take the examination. After the test, I had to call the office, like, twenty times for them to even agree to give me an interview for one of the positions, but I kept calling and bugging them.

Finally, they agreed to give me an interview, and I was excited. This was for a new "grant-funded" position (which basically meant no benefits of State employment, like no health insurance, pension, no job protection, etc.) for, like, $26,000 a year back in 2001. But I didn't care; I just wanted something more stable, and I knew that I would be fine if I could just get my foot in the door and prove how good I was. Well, that is exactly what happened, and you know what else happened? It was a job where I was paired with a police officer and worked directly with them in assisting first-time juvenile offenders and trying to get them to avoid having a juvenile record by completing the program. So see how God worked there; even though I didn't get to become a police officer, I worked with one in a police station. I even got a special license where I could drive the police cars—without lights and sirens, but it was cool just to do that. So I stayed in this position for a while, and they eventually gave me benefits, and my wife and I decided to purchase a town house together and would eventually get married. My mother-in-law even had to "co-sign" for the engagement ring because I didn't make enough money.

Moving out of my parents' house for good was very rewarding for me, because it meant that I finally did it against all odds: I made something of myself. My father was not happy for me and would make comments like, "Call me when you're making $50,000 a year." Also, not too long after I moved out of my parents' house for good, my mother also started to basically deteriorate from fibromyalgia and

MIKE'S TESTIMONY AND BACKGROUND

was told she was going to be on pain medication the rest of her life. After she had an incident because she was on so much morphine that her intestinal tracts basically went to sleep, she decided she couldn't take it any longer and committed suicide by saving up her pain pills and hoarding them and then taking them all at once in the back of her car somewhere. I was never able to see a note or anything, so I have no idea if that is true and why she took her life or not, as I was not speaking with my father or mother or brother during that time. I do have my suspicions that something else may have contributed towards her taking her life, but I guess I will never know until I am up in Heaven with God. I still don't speak to my father to this day, even though I had contacted him through writing a letter to him, basically forgiving him for what he had done and letting him know that I had been saved by God and completely changed as a person and, after twenty+ years of no communication, I was finally open to talking with him and shared all of my contact information with him. I know he received this letter, as my brother confirmed it, but I have never heard from him. He hasn't even met my kids, and they are both in high school now, soon to be in college, and he didn't come to my wedding, either (neither did my brother). The reason I sent this letter to my father was because on father's day weekend at my church the message delivered by the pastor was "you should reach out to your father to honor him, as the Bible says, even if you haven't spoken with him in a while." The pastor suggested even just writing a letter was a good first step, so that is what I did: I listened to God's message and did my part. Whether my earthly father ever contacts me again is up to him, and honestly, it's between him and God at this point, and I am at peace either way he decides, knowing I have done all that I can do.

After a few years into marriage, a buddy of mine signed us up for a real estate "investing" class that we thought was about how to buy and sell properties to make lots of cash. The real estate market was going absolutely nuts too back in 2005, so it was a good time to be getting in as an investor. The problem is when you are only making $26,000 a year and your spouse is making the same, how are you going to find any money to be able to invest in anything? AND it turns out that the "class" wasn't even about investing in the first place; it was about getting your real estate license to become a licensed real estate agent so you could affiliate with a broker and sell real estate to people. I went into it and said, "Well, I already paid for the class, so I may as well just get the license and see what it takes, and worst case I will sell just one house and break even and call it a day." Well, this is where my story takes a HUGE turn.

My first year in real estate, I was making more money with my State job probably closer to $32,000 now that

MIKE'S TESTIMONY AND BACKGROUND

I had benefits, but I sold, like, four homes, which made me, like, $20,000 (I was on an entry level 50/50 split at the time) in extra income. Then my next year, I sold, like, eight homes, so I was making more than my State job. So I said, "Let's just have some fun and see what happens." I wound up making three times my State salary the next year. Then the next year was even more than that. My wife and I had moved into a much larger home than our town home and then got pregnant and started our family with our kids. Eventually, I called my wife and said, "Why am I wasting all my time at my State job when I can be making real money in real estate?" So I decided to "retire" from my State job early and take a leap of faith into a 100% commission job that I had to pay to be at. Now, I didn't get anything from the State for that, but I will get a small pension from them when I hit sixty-two for my twelve years of service that I gave to them. But I didn't care because I finally found what I thought was my calling: to be the best real estate agent on the planet!

Real estate was just different, and I could feel it; it was almost like a drug for me where the sky was the limit and I would finally show my earth father that I never needed him or his help or any of his money! You see, once I decided I was going to be the best at real estate, I was on a mission to prove to everyone in the industry who I was, and I was going to do it on my own without a large team of agents.

Teams were a new thing that were starting in my industry where you had one really good agent at the head and then a bunch of other agents that would work with all of the "leads" that the large producing agent "generated" for them. I was producing and generating and working with and closing ALL of my own leads and started making some serious cash. I mean, hey, when you keep it small, you keep it all!

When I say serious cash, I am talking $750,000 to $800,000+ a year on my own in addition to flipping one to two homes a year, making an additional $50,000 on each of those at thirty-seven years old. To put it in perspective, that much money was thirteen to fifteen years' worth of what I would have made working for the State in one year. I had it all, so I bought my 9600+ square-foot dream home, had people making custom suits and clothing for me (dress shirts with my signature on the sleeves, sport coats with my name sewn into them, pants, jeans, shoes, ties, belts, etc.), people cutting my grass, people doing other landscaping projects for me, people cleaning my house—you name it, I had it, and I was unstoppable. I even paid ALL cash for a 14th floor, two-bedroom, two-bath condo down Ocean City, MD, in an oceanfront building, and we could see both the ocean and the bay (and sunrises over the ocean and sunsets over the bay every day) from our unit and even bought another investment/rental property, too (so I owned three homes at this point). The years just kept going, too, year after year, new record after new record in sales. I was unstoppable; I was INVINCIBLE! I was the number #1 agent at my entire sales brokerage in 2016, 2017, 2018 and #2 in 2019. When you are running 250MPH, seven days a week, things eventually got pretty stressful, so you had to take care of yourself (mind, body, and spirit). So I decided I needed to de-stress and decided to self medicate myself with some marijuana just like I did when I was a teenager, just to relax a little bit (calm the nerves). Now what is important to note here is that making the kind of cash I was making also connected me to people who knew people who could get me whatever I wanted. I knew people who owned the medical dispensaries before smoking marijuana became legalized in Maryland, so I got the best, most POTENT stuff on the shelf to smoke. For about a year, I would go out almost every night into my garage and light up my bong and take hit after hit of 35% to 40% THC potency and then go upstairs completely numb to the world, enjoy some television and music, and pass out. At my peak usage, towards the end of my usage, I was taking in excess of 30 (that is NOT a typo) bong hits a night just to get the tiniest bit stoned of the most potent marijuana on the market because I was INVINCIBLE! At that point in my life, I probably even thought I was my own God, and I was actually in the best shape of my life as well as I was eating very clean (putting freshly squeezed grapefruits into my bottled water) and going to the gym five to six days a week. In fact, towards the end of my usage, I would often get high before I even went to the gym to work out because I found I would be able to lift heavier weights if my muscles didn't actually feel the resistance. Basically if you saw the movie the Wolf of Wall Street, that was me, just slightly less money and selling real estate instead of stocks.

So guess who didn't like me smoking the "devils lettuce" (marijuana) and decided enough was enough? Good old God did! And even at this point, I wasn't a believer in what was actually going on and just how blessed I was. In fact, I had literally NO FRICKIN idea what was going on because of all the marijuana I had been smoking. So here is what God let happen...

He let the devil mess with me and make me so paranoid that my wife was out to get me and was actually going to hire a hit man to kill me for the life insurance money. But God also was inside of my head as well. You see, I prayed for God to help me and save me of all the paranoid thoughts and feelings going on. God said to me (literally spoke to me in my head and told me) to get rid of all of my marijuana stuff, bongs, drugs that were left over, etc. and told me to throw them out and assured me I would never have a craving for it ever again in my lifetime. I was leaving that morning for a trip down to our condo in Ocean City, MD, to just try to relax for a few days by myself as everyone thought that was what I needed. I literally turned on the radio and started driving to the beach but had to stop at my real estate office first. On the radio, every single song spoke to me with the lyrics, and I would ask questions to the radio (literally talking to it out loud), and the next song would come on, and the title would be an answer to the question I just asked. I got to my office and threw all the drugs out, talked to my assistant, and then left for the beach. As I continued to drive down the highway, I kept seeing billboards about Jesus Saves and suicides and had no idea what it meant, but literally, Jesus billboards were everywhere. I stopped in a fast food restaurant to get two cheeseburgers because I was starving, and up on the TV in the corner was a television talk show on, and the line on the bottom of the screen said, "Why women hire hitmen to kill their husbands." I freaked out at this point and got super panicked. I thought everyone in there was watching me; I didn't know what was going on at the time. However, NOW I DO KNOW that was the devil messing with me.

Eventually, the devil continued messing with me while I was in a mall getting my haircut, doing some shopping before I went to the beach, and I became a distraction to people in the mall (I even walked up to one man in a wheel chair who was wearing a necklace with a cross on it and told him I could help him walk if he just took my hand) that they contacted mall security and had me sit down in an area by myself. They contacted the police department and had me transported to a local hospital for an emergency petition evaluation for my health.

What happened to me that day was the beginning of a spiritual awakening, although I didn't know it at the time. It was a spiritual awakening, and that was the feeling of the Holy Spirit inside of me because when I got to the hospital and they kept me there for a day or two for an evaluation, I remember reading through magazines and pointing out the negative big company ads for drug manufacturers and how they were just deceiving people with their ads to make a bigger profit and even noticing that the screws in the doors and door frames looked like little crosses. And I am not even lying when I tell you that the next day they had someone come down and remove all of the screws that looked like crosses and replaced them with screws that did not look like crosses any more. And I was in complete absolute peace while there, not a care in the world, literally feeling just like being in Heaven on earth requesting to watch the television channel that had peaceful music with photos of nature on it. And I can remember being interviewed by some psychiatric staff at the hospital and testing them to see if they believed in God before I would agree to even

MIKE'S TESTIMONY AND BACKGROUND

speak with them.

I finally wound up at a psychiatric inpatient facility for the first time in my life, and I was still having the feeling of the Holy Spirit inside of me, and it's a good thing too, because there were some extremely evil and dangerous spirits at the new facility that I was transported to. In this facility, you had roommates, and my first roommate would mess with me by leaving out colored pictures and puzzles for me to complete or leave a book turned to a certain page for me to read, all very spiritual-related, almost like I was on a quest of some kind. I eventually went a little crazy in there (as most people do in a psychiatric facility) and ripped a toilet out of the wall due to not knowing if who I was dealing with was the evil spirits or the good spirits in the facility. Once I finally got "drugged up" on some extremely heavy psychiatric medications, they eventually would be in a position to release me from the facility, and my wife described me as a literal walking zombie when she picked me up. Everything was gone: my personality, my drive, my confidence, everything, and now I was gonna be on these drugs for my "bipolar" condition for the rest of my life, I was told. There was so much stuff that happened inside of that facility, phone calls that I made, things I said, things I did, things I had to do just to survive. If you don't believe in the devil, go to a psychiatric facility and stay there with no access to the outside world for fourteen days.

I think you will start believing in the evil that is out there.

Now, I need to say this here, and there is no other way I can say it other than I have the BEST WIFE ON THE PLANET! Anyone who would stay with someone like me that just put her through what I did is a Saint! So we went on to our new lives with me being like a zombie on all of these bipolar medications that basically stripped me of having a personality at all, having any creativity at all, having any drive at all, and having any motivation at all and—to make things even better—made me gain on average 20lbs a year for the next five years. Every year for the next five years, my income slowly dropped to $400,000 to $300,000 to $150,000 to $72,000 to not having a check come in for six months. Now I was 100lbs more than I was, not making any money, not having any drive, creativity, motivation, or personality; this is where the depression and complete darkness really started to set in.

I did see this possibly coming though as my income started to slowly slip away, so back in June of 2023, I decided to take a handgun class to get my permit so I could legally purchase a handgun. I did eventually purchase a handgun later in 2023 or early 2024. I honestly don't even know what kind of a gun I bought, only that it was the same gun that most police officers used, so I figured if it worked for them it would work for me. I am not a gun person, have never owned one, and have probably only shot one, like, once or twice in my life when I was a kid staying with a friend of mine with his father. Having the gun literally scared the death out of me each time I thought about shooting it or even touching it.

Now, we still had plenty of money in the bank to get us through for a while and also had plenty in investment and retirement accounts that we could go to if we had to, but it had been six months of no commission. That hadn't happened to me, the king of real estate, since it was my first year in the business twenty years ago when I had another job with income coming in. I also knew I really had no other options; I mean, once you are self-employed for twenty years, you are basically off the grid and out of the workforce, so where would I go that I can make $200,000+ at an entry level job? I knew I had a $2,000,000 insurance policy on my life, so at least my wife would get that and could take care of everything is where my mind was. And the voice inside of my head the whole time was telling me, "You will never make any money again; you are a terrible real estate agent; look at you, no drive, no personality, no creativity; how can you expect to make any money, LOSER; you should just kill yourself and get it over with." It was all from the devil and from the darkness that surrounded me that I was so deep in. And months would go by, and I would find another reason to push it off: Sometimes it was a birthday; sometimes it was a holiday (Halloween, Thanksgiving, Christmas, etc.); sometimes it was even something like the Ravens' season not being over yet with a chance to go to the Superbowl.

After several months of NO INCOME WHATSOEVER, I finally went outside one night, and I lit up a cigarette (yes, I was smoking cigarettes again), and I looked up to the blackened sky, the stars, the moon, and I cried out to God! I said, "IF YOU ARE F***N REAL, then GOD SAVE ME! I need you to fix me financially. I need you to fix my family. I need you to fix me; I'm broken, and I don't know what to do anymore." And I said, "If you don't fix me, I am just going to fix myself with the gun I have, and it's all going to be over." I basically threatened Him at the time. I told Him that I was sorry for anything and everything I had ever done in my life that I wasn't supposed to do. I told Him that, if he saved me, I promised that I would do anything He wanted me to do in the future. And I basically completely surrendered my life over to Him at that point.

Wouldn't you know it, the very next day I woke up, and BOOM, creativity was back, motivation was back, personality was back (even though I didn't know it yet), and that feeling in my heart was back. The same feeling I had five years prior when I went "crazy" during my "bipolar" event and that I wound up going into the medical facility for. *Finally,* I thought. "Finally, this is here; this spiritual awakening is here, and I have the Holy Spirit again!" And boy did I have that Holy Spirit. I flushed all of my "bi-polar" medications down the toilet that I was supposed to take because I already knew that God had fixed me, and I did not have bi-polar and, in fact, never did. I threw out my cigarettes; I started eating better and started making more positive changes in my life all at once. Well, a few days later, my wife started to realize some changes in my "energy" and thought I needed to go back to my psychiatrist's office to make sure I was taking enough medications. I fought her on that and said I didn't need to see him before I finally gave in and said I would be happy to see him. I went into that appointment with him and told him that he would never know how I feel. I told him my story and told him he would never make as much money as I did and he also wouldn't ever know what it's like to go from that level of income to no money for six months coming in. I also asked him if he happened to believe in God to which he NEVER REPLIED. Once I saw that, I told him I would be in the lobby waiting for the police to pick me up so that they could take me to the hospital to be re-evaluated to determine if I was a danger to myself or others and having another "manic" episode due to my "bi-polar" disorder. I also told him he should lock up everyone who went to church on Easter Sunday because they believe in

God like me. I also told him that one day he would have to answer for what he has done for not believing me and instead misdiagnosing me.

Once at the hospital, I was interviewed by several nurses, all of whom I was very pleasant to and thanked for doing their jobs. At this point, I knew the program well and what they needed me to do. While I was waiting for my nurse to come back to my room in the ER, there was a man who was brought in who was screaming, and I mean *screaming*—like, disturbing the entire ER. I said to the two people monitoring me outside of my room, "Do you know why he is screaming?" They said they did not. I told them that he had a demon inside of him, and until he said, "God, help me" or "God, I give up," he would keep screaming, and it was going to get louder and louder. Sure enough, it got very loud, and then he said, "God I give up," and the screaming stopped immediately. They both looked at each other in disbelief and then at me. I told them the Spirit told me that. Even after all that, the nurses decided that I needed to go to another psychiatric unit only because I had an "episode" five years prior. What is convenient is that the hospital and psychiatric facility are all under the same umbrella, so everyone was making money off of me (side note).

So this $28,000 trip to the psychiatric facility was better than the last one because this time I knew exactly what was going on, and I had the Holy Spirit inside of me ON FIRE in my heart. I went in, guns blazing, telling the demons to come out because I was "ready" for them this time. You see, I had God, and I knew it! Even before I had any scriptures or knew what was in the Bible, the Spirit told me what I needed to know. The Spirit told me not to be afraid because "no weapon formed against me would prosper" (Isaiah 54:17). The Spirit gave me the confidence to walk around in that facility like I owned the place! There were very evil spirits there with me, but when I had the Spirit the way I did, I was scared of NONE of it. All I kept thinking was a song that was in my head from the rock band Skillet called Invincible. I highly encourage you all to play that song; it really pumps me up, especially during weight training work outs (just google it on YouTube). You see, I felt completely INVINCIBLE, just like I did when I was at the top of my game on drugs, only this time, there were no drugs and instead it was the Holy Spirit making me feel like this. I needed that too, because the devil himself was in this psychiatric facility, trying to break me down. I even had a guy who looked just like Charlie Manson: hair, beard, and all, staying in the room right next to mine, and I caught him in my room several times during my stay messing with my things when I was in the main group open area. I didn't sleep for more than twenty minutes for seven days straight, and I kept telling the doctors it was because I had the Spirit inside of me, yet no one would believe me. I refused to take all medications for seven days as well; they said they had never seen anyone like me and were planning on taking me to court to force me to take my medications if I continued to refuse, even though I was there voluntarily. Eventually, I prayed to God about the medications, and He advised that I should take the medications as He would not let them harm me at all. So I started taking the medications to get released from there. While I was there, not only did I fight demons and evil spirits, but I also helped all of the other patients at the facility with their issues. Some of them were so severely mentally disturbed that they couldn't even speak and were a little scary to look at, but I still sat with them, talked with them, colored with them (with my purple crayons), ate with them, prayed with them (especially before meals), and watched television with them too. In fact, everyone was doing so much better when I was there with them on the unit, and I even heard that from some of the staff on the unit too; they couldn't believe how well everyone was doing while I was there.

Finally, they let me go home on my 46th birthday, April 8, 2024, the day of the strong solar eclipse. My wife came to pick me up again, just like she did from the last facility. I truly don't know what I have done to deserve her and her love. I told her when we first moved in together that she was my earth angel sent here to save me and rescue me from my parents' house. She has been through a lot because of me and the choices I have made and has kept it together the entire time, especially at home with both of our kids.

From the minute I came home this time, I was drawn to Jesus and to the Bible. I immediately got involved in two different Bible study Men's groups and soon after got involved with a Celebrate Recovery program through a local church that I attended as well. I also started going to church every Sunday and from there got introduced to three more Bible Study groups that I have participated with. Through these groups, I have learned some of the Bible (I still have A LOT more to learn), and it has made me much closer to God. I have also started my own, very amateur podcast on YouTube where I interview people about how they came to find God for some real-life testimonials that others can see on the internet. I realized it was a challenge to find people on a regular basis who were comfortable enough to talk about their personal relationships with God "on camera," so I thought, "Well then, I need to fill the episodes with some other kind of content as the show must go on." So I started to pray about it, and now God sends me messages through the Spirit on what to talk about. Sometimes it is a topic, sometimes it is scripture, sometimes it is a song, and sometimes I don't even know what I will be doing until I start talking, and the Spirit just takes over inside of me, almost like directing me on exactly what to say.

I typically pray at least two times per day, once in the morning as well as once at night right before I go to bed. There is no right or wrong way to pray; all you have to do is talk to God. Talk about your good stuff, talk about your bad stuff; ask for wisdom, guidance, knowledge, clarity, and discernment. I even talk to Him when it's just me and Him, like when I am just driving down the road in my car. He communicates regularly with me as well and even makes me laugh sometimes as he has quite the sense of humor with what he does to you and for you in this crazy life. And it literally took me until today while writing this part of the book to realize all of the Jesus Saves billboards and Suicide hotline number billboards that I saw five years ago were to plant them in my mind as a preview (almost like a vision) for where I was going to be five years later and that I would need Him to "SAVE ME" like He did. It was just like everything I went through was pre-destined or pre-ordained or pre-planned by God. Nothing in life happens by accident, by coincidence, or by mistake. Instead, EVERYTHING happens for a reason, and sometimes only God knows what that reason is. I believe it took me five years because I am extremely hard-headed, even when I was in a zombie-like state. You see, God took away my income little by little, year after year, almost like saying to me each year, "Have you had enough yet" And it took me getting to the point where he took it all from me, no sales commission and no money coming in for six months, to finally get me to break and run to Him just like He wanted me to do in the first place during the first time. But I let my own ego and pride get in the way; even after going through what I initially did with my first psychiatric stay, I still thought I was the one who got myself through all of that, and I actually believed the doctors when they told me I had bi-polar disorder. It wasn't until when I finally ran to God and asked Him to save me, to fix me, to heal me that I finally realized the very next day that I was HEALED COMPLETELY, HEAD TO TOE! Miracles do happen, and it happened to me, so now I had to keep up with my end of the bargain and do whatever God wanted me to do for the rest of my life.

I have turned my life over to God as well as to Jesus and the Holy Spirit and live my life according to the scriptures and what God wants us to do while we are here to the absolute best of my ability. As I am writing this part of the book, I am getting ready to get baptized this Sunday, October 27, 2024, and can't wait as it will be the first time many of my friends and family have been to my "new" church for a service. I absolutely cannot wait to officially be born again with Jesus! Do I mess up sometimes? Sure, but then I REPENT and simply ask God for forgiveness! But if I know something is wrong, I NEVER do it, EVER, not anymore!

SO HOW DO YOU START YOUR JOURNEY WITH JESUS?

Repentance in the Bible is a process of changing one's mind and heart about a past action or attitude and turning away from it in favor of a more righteous path. In Acts 3:19, it states, "Repent, then, and turn to God, so that your sins may be wiped out, that times of refreshing may come from the Lord."

The first step towards your own personal salvation so you can start to take your journey with Jesus is to repent fully for everything you have ever done wrong. Chances are, if you have never fully repented before, it could be a very long time for you to actually sit down and repent for everything you have ever done wrong. So I would say start with the BIG STUFF: you know, stuff like breaking the ten commandments, then the littler stuff until you get down to things you are completely forgetting about. Then just simply say, "...and ANYTHING else that I may have forgotten to mention that I need to repent for."

ARE YOU GOING TO HEAVEN OR HELL?

This is your opportunity to sit down with God and give it to Him, let Him really know everything that you are apologizing for. Here's the reality: He already knows everything you have already done anyway, so it isn't like anything is going to be a surprise to Him. Once you are finished apologizing, beg Him to forgive you for everything you have done. After that, then it's time to ask Him to "SAVE" you. Let Him know that you are now ready to start your journey with Jesus or your walk with Jesus or your adventure with Jesus. As you can see, this step barely takes up two pages in this entire book, yet it's crucial to get you to be able to start your journey/walk/adventure with Jesus. The best part is this is 100% free, and it's something that you can do in the comfort of your own home whenever it's convenient for you. I recommend you go to a quiet place in your home where you are by yourself (no kids, no pets, no nothing), just you and God and maybe a candle or something like that. Then just start talking to God. It may be hard to do at first, but with time, it will become easier and easier to do. Just start with something simple like three things you are grateful for. It amazes me sometimes, I meet people who say they are not grateful for three things, and I am like, don't we have five senses? Aren't you at least thankful for three of the five, like hearing, seeing, and feeling? Start there, then get into apologizing to God for not knowing any better and telling Him that you want to be part of His world and you want Him to be a part of your

SO HOW DO YOU START YOUR JOURNEY WITH JESUS?

world. Tell Him you are ready to change your ways, you are ready to change your life, you are ready for Him to show you the way. Then here comes the BIG PART: tell Him you are ready to fully SURRENDER yourself over to Him. An analogy I always like to use here is pretend you are a car and you give the keys to God and tell Him, "Take me wherever you want to go; drive me through the mud, the sand, the dirt, the stone, the pavement, wherever." God wants you to fully surrender your entire life over to Him. It is scary at first to realize you will not have any control any longer over your income, reputation, ego, or pride. Thankfully, you also will no longer have to deal with other things like fear, anxiety, worry, depression, and many other mental health conditions. Remember, you give EVERYTHING to God, not just the good stuff, but ALL of your problems too. It is also important to remember that you need to continue to SURRENDER your will to God EVERY SINGLE DAY. Once you have fully surrendered to God, then you can start to focus on living your life like Jesus would. In fact, there is an entire section in the Bible that covers this exact topic, and it's one of Jesus' famous speeches called "The Sermon on the Mount." You can find it located in Matthew Chapters 5-7, and I feel so strongly about it that I am going to insert it right here into the book so you have it more readily available:

Matthew Chapter 5: "Now when Jesus saw the crowds, he went up on a mountainside and sat down. His disciples came to him, and he began to teach them. He said, 'Blessed are the poor in spirit, for theirs is the kingdom of heaven. Blessed are those who mourn, for they will be comforted. Blessed are the meek, for they will inherit the earth. Blessed are those who hunger and thirst for righteousness, for they will be filled. Blessed are the merciful, for they will be shown mercy. Blessed are the pure heart, for they will see God. Blessed are the peacemakers, for they will be called children of God. Blessed are those who are persecuted because of righteousness, for theirs is the kingdom of heaven. Blessed are you when people insult you, persecute you and falsely say all kinds of evil against you because of me. Rejoice and be glad, because great is your reward in heaven, for in the same way they persecuted the prophets who were before you. You are the salt of the earth. But if the salt loses its saltiness, how can it be made salty again? It is no longer good for anything, except to be thrown out and trampled underfoot. You are the light of the world. A town built on a hill cannot be hidden. Neither do people light a lamp and put it under a bowl. Instead they put it on its stand and it gives light to everyone in the house. In the same way, let your light shine before others, that they may see your good deeds and glorify your Father in heaven. Do not think that I have come to abolish the Law or the Prophets; I have not come to abolish them but to fulfill them. For truly I tell you, until heaven and earth disappear, not the smallest letter, not the least stroke of

SO HOW DO YOU START YOUR JOURNEY WITH JESUS?

a pen, will by any means disappear from the Law until everything is accomplished. Therefore anyone who sets aside one of the least of these commands and teaches others accordingly will be called least in the kingdom of heaven, but whoever practices and teaches these commands will be called great in the kingdom of heaven. For I tell you that unless your righteousness surpasses that of the Pharisees and the teachers of the law, you will certainly not enter the kingdom of heaven. You have heard that it was said to the people long ago, "You shall not murder, and anyone who murders will be subject to judgment." But I tell you that anyone who is angry with a brother or sister will be subject to judgment. Again, anyone who says to a brother or sister, "Raca," is answerable to the court. And anyone who says, "You fool!" will be in danger of the fire of hell. Therefore, if you are offering your gift at the altar and there remember that your brother or sister has something against you, leave your gift there in front of the altar. First go and be reconciled to them; then come and offer your gift. Settle matters quickly with your adversary who is taking you to court. Do it while you are still together on the way, or your adversary may hand you over to the judge, and the judge may hand you over to the officer, and you may be thrown into prison. Truly I tell you, you will not get out until you have paid the last penny. You have heard that it was said, "You shall not commit adultery." But I tell you that anyone who looks at a woman lustfully has already committed adultery with her in his heart. If your right eye causes you to stumble, gouge it out and throw it away. It is better for you to lose one part of your body than for your whole body to be thrown into hell. And if your right hand causes you to stumble, cut it off and throw it away. It is better for you to lose one part of your body than for your whole body to go into hell. It has been said, "Anyone who divorces his wife must give her a certificate of divorce." But I tell you that anyone who divorces his wife, except for sexual immorality, makes her the victim of adultery, and anyone who marries a divorced woman commits adultery. Again, you have heard that it was said to the people long ago, "Do not break your oath, but fulfill to the Lord the vows you have made." But I tell you, do not swear an oath at all: either by heaven, for it is God's throne; or by the earth, for it is his footstool; or by Jerusalem, for it is the city of the Great King. And do not swear by your head, for you cannot make even one hair white or black. All you need to say is simply "Yes" or "No"; anything beyond this comes from the evil one. You have heard that it was said, "Eye for eye, and tooth for tooth." But I tell you, do not resist an evil person. If anyone slaps you on the right cheek, turn to them the other cheek also. And if anyone wants to sue you and take your shirt, hand over your coat as well. If anyone forces you to go one mile, go with them two miles. Give to the one who asks you, and do not turn away from the one who wants to borrow from you. You have heard that it was said, "Love your neighbor and hate your enemy." But I tell you, love your enemies and pray for those who persecute you, that you may be children of your Father in heaven. He causes his sun to rise on the evil and the good, and sends rain on the righteous and the unrighteous. If you love those who love you, what reward will you get? Are not even the tax collectors doing that? And if you greet only your own people, what are you doing more than others? Do not even pagans do that? Be perfect, therefore, as your heavenly Father is perfect.'"

Matthew Chapter 6: "'Be careful not to practice your righteousness in front of others to be seen by them. If you do, you will have no reward from your Father in heaven. So when you give to the needy, do not announce it with trumpets, as the hypocrites do in the synagogues and on the streets, to be honored by others. Truly I tell you, they have received their reward in full. But when you give to the needy, do not let your left hand know what your right hand is doing, so that your giving may be in secret. Then you Father, who sees what is done in secret, will reward you. And when you pray, do not be like the hypocrites, for they love to pray standing in the synagogues and on the street corners to be seen by others. Truly I tell you, they have received their reward in full. But when you pray, go into your room, close the door and pray to your Father, who is unseen. Then your Father, who sees what is done in secret, will reward you. And when you pray, do not keep on babbling like pagans, for they think they will be heard because of their many words. Do not be like them, for your Father knows what you need before you ask him. This, then, is how you should pray: "Our Father in heaven, hallowed be your name, your kingdom come, your will be done, on earth as it is in heaven. Give us today our daily bread. And forgive us our debts, as we also have forgiven our debtors. And lead us not into temptation, but deliver us from the evil one." For if you forgive other people when they sin against you, your heavenly Father will also forgive you. But if you do not forgive others their sins, your Father will not forgive your sins. When you fast, do not look somber as the hypocrites do, for they disfigure their faces to show others they are fasting. Truly I tell you, they have received their reward in full. But when you fast, put oil on your head and wash your face, so that it will not be obvious to others that you are fasting, but only to your Father, who is unseen; and your Father, who sees what is done in secret, will reward you. Do not store up for yourselves treasures on earth, where moths and vermin destroy, and where thieves break in and steal. But store up for yourselves treasures in heaven, where moths and vermin do not destroy, and where thieves do not break in and steal. For where your treasure is, there your heart will be also. The eye is the lamp of the body. If your eyes are healthy, your whole body will be full of light. But if your eyes are unhealthy, your whole body will be full of darkness. If then the light within you is

SO HOW DO YOU START YOUR JOURNEY WITH JESUS?

darkness, how great is that darkness! No one can serve two masters. Either you will hate the one and love the other, or you will be devoted to the one and despise the other. You cannot serve both God and money. Therefore I tell you, do not worry about your life, what you will eat or drink, or about your body, what you will wear. Is not life more than food, and the body more than clothes? Look at the birds of the air; they do not sow or reap or store away in barns, and yet your heavenly Father feeds them. Are you not much more valuable than they? Can any one of you by worrying add a single hour to your life? And why do you worry about clothes? See how the flowers of the field grow. They do not labor or spin. Yet I tell you that not even Solomon in all his splendor was dressed like one of these. If that is how God clothes the grass of the field, which is here today and tomorrow is thrown into the fire, will he not much more clothe you; you of little faith? So do not worry, saying, "What shall we eat?" or "What shall we drink?" or "What shall we wear?" For the pagans run after all these things, and your heavenly Father knows that you need them. But seek first his kingdom and his righteousness, and all these things will be given to you as well. Therefore do not worry about tomorrow, for tomorrow will worry about itself. Each day has enough trouble of its own.'"

Matthew Chapter 7: "'Do not judge, or you too will be judged. For in the same way you judge others, you will be judged, and with the measure you use, it will be measured to you. Why do you look at the speck of sawdust in your brother's eye and pay no attention to the plank in your own eye? How can you say to your brother, "Let me take the speck out of your eye," when all the time there is a plank in your own eye? You hypocrite, first take the plank out of your own eye, and then you will see clearly to remove the speck from your brother's eye. Do not give dogs what is sacred; do not throw your pearls to pigs. If you do, they may trample them under their feet, and turn and tear you to pieces. Ask and it will be given to you; seek and you will find; knock and the door will be opened to you. For everyone who asks receives; the one who seeks finds; and to the one who knocks, the door will be opened. Which of you, if your son asks for bread, will give him a stone? Or if he asks for a fish, will give him a snake? If you, then, though you are evil, know how to give good gifts to your children, how much more will your Father in heaven give good gifts to those who ask him! So in everything, do to others what you would have them do to you, for this sums up the Law and the Prophets. Enter through the narrow gate. For wide is the gate and broad is the road that leads to destruction, and many enter through it. But small is the gate and narrow the road that leads to life, and only a few find it. Watch out for false prophets. They come to you in sheep's clothing, but inwardly they are ferocious wolves. By their fruit you will recognize them. Do people pick grapes from thornbushes, or figs from thistles? Likewise, every good tree bears good fruit, but a bad tree bears bad fruit. A good tree cannot bear bad fruit, and a bad tree cannot bear good fruit. Every tree that does not bear good fruit is cut down and thrown into the fire. They by their fruit you will recognize them. *Not everyone who says to me, "Lord, Lord," will enter the kingdom of heaven, but only the one who does the will of my Father who is in heaven* [bold added]. Many will say to me on that day, "Lord, Lord, did we not prophesy in your name and in your name drive out demons and in your name perform many miracles?" Then I will tell them plainly, "I never knew you." Away from me, you evildoers! Therefore, everyone who hears these words of mine and puts them into practice is like a wise man who built his house on the rock. The rain came down, the streams rose, and the winds blew and beat against the house; yet it did not fall, because it had its foundation on the rock. But everyone who hears these words of mine and does not put them into practice is like a foolish man who built his house on sand. The rains came down, the streams rose, and the winds blew and beat against that house, and it fell with a great crash.' When Jesus had finished saying these things, the crowds were amazed at his teaching, because he taught as one who had authority, and not as their teachers of the law."

I know that was A LOT of scripture to be added into a book like this, but there are just so many pearls of wisdom contained in that sermon that Jesus spoke, and it really should be used as a rough guide for how you should live your life practicing the way of Jesus. He specifically talks about so many different things in life and how you are supposed to handle them and react to them. You should also obviously follow the Ten Commandments that were written by God as well. And again for reference, just so you have it handy, I am going to list the Ten Commandments below, which can also be found under Exodus 20 in the NIV Bible:

"And God spoke these words: 'I am the LORD your God, who brought you out of Egypt, out of the land of slavery. You shall have no other gods before me. You shall not make for yourself an image in the form of anything in heaven above or on the earth beneath or in the waters below. You shall not bow down to them or worship them; for I, the LORD your God, am a jealous God, punishing the children for the sin of the parents to the third and fourth generation of those who hate me, but showing love to a thousand generations of those who love me and keep my commandments. You shall not misuse the name of the LORD your God, for the LORD will not hold anyone guiltless who misuses his name. Remember the Sabbath day by keeping it holy. Six days you shall labor and do all your work, but the seventh day is a Sabbath to the LORD your God. On it you shall not do any work, neither you, nor your son or daughter, nor your male or female servant, nor your animals, nor any foreigner residing in your towns. For in six days the LORD made the heavens and the earth, the sea, and all that is in them, but he rested on the seventh day.

SO HOW DO YOU START YOUR JOURNEY WITH JESUS?

Therefore the LORD blessed the Sabbath day and made it holy. Honor your father and your mother, so that you may live long in the land the LORD your God is giving you. You shall not murder. You shall not commit adultery. You shall not steal. You shall not give false testimony against your neighbor. You shall not covet your neighbor's house. You shall not covet your neighbor's wife, or his male or female servant, his ox or donkey, or anything that belongs to your neighbor.'"

Now I want to make a suggestion about seeking another book that may help you with living your new life as an apprentice or disciple of Jesus. Before I tell you about the book, I want to tell you how I got the book in my hands. I was doing an open house on a property in a 55+ community (which means you have to be at least 55 years old to live and purchase a home there), and it was a pretty amazing day. Business had been pretty slow for me lately in the real estate world, but I felt the need to be out there in the trenches to try to sell this particular home and also maybe pick up some new clients along the way. So the first person that came into the open house that day blew me away. You see, there is this "retirement community," which I will not name here, and my wife actually used to work with them. They get a tremendous amount of people who move into their community who have homes that they need to sell. While my wife was working there, I was always told I couldn't be on their preferred agent list because it was a "conflict of interest." Well, once my wife "retired" from there and was no longer working, I again approached, and this time they let me be on their preferred list. However, I never really got much business from them as business always seemed to go to three particular agents all the time, and no one else ever got an opportunity. It got so bad that many agents in the industry feel like there was some kind of an illegal kickback fee getting paid to the sales reps in the community who were referring out all the business to these three particular agents.

Well, it just so happened that the first visitor at my open house was the sales DIRECTOR for the retirement community—I mean the boss of the sales reps. I couldn't believe that out of all the houses they could have visited, they picked mine. I believe God sent him there for me to meet with and talk with since I had been trying so hard to get more business referrals from them. I talked with him for about thirty-five minutes and toured the home with him and his wife. They were very nice people and actually did wind up putting in a contract on the property using their own agent a few days later, but we wound up taking a different contract instead in the end.

Now, back to how I got the book. Well, after a steady visit of about eight different prospective buyers, it got quiet, and I was just kind of standing in the kitchen going through my social media feed, and someone came into the

SO HOW DO YOU START YOUR JOURNEY WITH JESUS?

door. Turns out it was a neighbor about seventy-five years old who just wanted to stop by. He immediately pointed to my necklace, which is a cross, and said, "What's the deal with that?" I told him, "I am a strong believer in God and Jesus and the Holy Spirit," and he then told me, "Well, then I have two books you need to buy." I swear when he said that, I felt like God was talking to me. Then I pulled out my phone and asked him what the names of the books were so I could text them to myself. Then he grabbed my phone and said, "Here I will just text it for you to make sure you get them correctly." The books were both written by the same author, John Mark Comer. The first book was called *Practicing the Way, Be with Jesus, Become like him, Do as he did*. The second book was called *The Ruthless Elimination of Hurry*.

If you are serious about starting your journey/walk/adventure with Jesus, I HIGHLY RECOMMEND you get the *Practicing the Way* book. There is so much good stuff in there from cover to cover that will help you in your journeys. I have since purchased almost every book that John Mark Comer has written and am in the process of reading them each one by one now. As you can imagine, since the open house was on a Sunday, the very next day on Monday I ordered the books and am so glad I did. But it was like God told me to order those two books as I needed to read them at that exact time. Normally when you read a book, you don't get a recommendation for another person's book in the middle from another author, but I believe in paying it forward, and it is information that is so important to so many of you out there. To be fully transparent, I will not get one dime from John Mark Comer for any of his sales of his book, *Practicing the Way,* and I don't want any either. Instead, maybe I will just get to meet with him one day over a cup of good coffee.

Okay, now it's time to learn how to practice the way of Jesus and how to live your lives like Him. Now you have the scriptures that you need to follow as your firm foundation, and you know the word of the LORD, but now it's time to start LIVING the word of the LORD! This is where it's all about your behavior, actions, choices, and building your obedience, loyalty, and trust between you and God. This doesn't happen overnight; you don't just wake up one day, and all of the sudden, you are living in this complete peace-like state in the world. Instead, it is a process of learning and growing with God leading the way. This is where you need to start believing that there are absolutely no coincidences in life and that everything in life happens for a reason, although you don't always know what that reason is. I will assure you there is ALWAYS a reason; it just takes time for us humans to understand WHY something happened to us sometimes. Remember, God is in total control over our lives, and He knows our blueprints inside and out. He knows exactly what we are capable of and what we are not capable of (and He can make changes

SO HOW DO YOU START YOUR JOURNEY WITH JESUS?

to make us capable if we are lacking). God wants what is absolutely best for us. He wants us to achieve our biggest dreams and desires and is here to help us do it if we work with Him in the right way. There are rules, like DO NOT SIN, follow the Commandments, listen to the instructions in the Sermon on the Mount, and live in the Spirit and not in the flesh.

Let's talk about living in the Spirit instead of the flesh and exactly what that means. I stumbled across Romans Chapter 8 one day while scrolling through my Facebook feed like I always do, and this passage really SPOKE to me, specifically verses 1-17. Again, I am going to put it here so it is readily available for reference to you:

Life Through the Spirit – Romans 8:1-17

"Therefore, there is now no condemnation for those who are in Christ Jesus, because through Christ Jesus the law of the Spirit who gives life has set you free from the law of sin and death. For what the law was powerless to do because it was weakened by the flesh, God did by sending his own Son in the likeness of sinful flesh to be a sin offering. And so he condemned sin in the flesh, in order that righteous requirement of the law might be fully met in us, who do not live according to the flesh but according to the Spirit. Those who live according to the flesh have their minds set on what the flesh desires; but those who live in accordance with the Spirit have their minds set on what the Spirit desires. The mind governed by the flesh is death, but the mind governed by the Spirit is life and peace. The mind governed by the flesh is hostile to God; it does not submit to God's law, nor can it do so. Those who are in the realm of the flesh cannot please God. You, however are not in the realm of the flesh but are in the realm of the Spirit, if indeed the Spirit of God lives in you. And if anyone does not have the Spirit of Christ, they do not belong to Christ. But if Christ is in you, then even though your body is subject to death because of sin, the Spirit gives life because of righteousness. And if the Spirit of him who raised Jesus from the dead is living in you, he who raised Christ from the dead will also give life to your mortal bodies because of his Spirit who lives in you. Therefore, brothers and sisters, we have an obligation—but it is not to the flesh, to live according to it. For if you live according to the flesh, you will die; but if by the Spirit you put to death the misdeeds of the body, you will live. For those who are led by the Spirit of God are the children of God. The Spirit you received does not make you slaves, so that you live in fear again; rather, the Spirit you received brought about your adoption to sonship. And by him we cry, 'Abba, Father.' The Spirit himself testifies with our spirit that we are God's children. Now if we are children, then we are heirs—heirs of God and co-heirs with Christ, if indeed we share in his sufferings in order that we may also share in his glory."

SO HOW DO YOU START YOUR JOURNEY WITH JESUS?

I know this Bible talk can get complicated, and we can tend to overthink some things here, but let's try to keep it simple. Now, imagine sitting on your sofa and watching television. Now, imagine that Jesus is sitting there with you on the sofa; is it going to make you change what you are watching on the television? In other words, because Jesus is there with you, would it make you re-think your decisions? This is how living in the Spirit is. You already have the Spirit in your heart, assuming you have repented all of your sins and asked God to save you. When you live in the Spirit, you basically live with Jesus being your co-pilot, whether that is in your car, at lunch, at work, in the park, at the gym, at your kids sports practice, at home, or really in anything you do. It is being cognizant that He is there with you, and you really need to do as He wants you to do and make the "right choices." That is really as simple as you can make it.

It also says in James 2:26, "For just as the body without the spirit is dead, so also faith without works is dead." So if you see someone who is in need of something somewhere, HELP THEM; get them whatever it is that they need. As it says in 2 Corinthians 9:7, "God loveth a cheerful giver." Bottom line: Be like the wise man and build your house on the rock and listen to the Lord's instructions for how to live your life.

NOW, WHY IS IT IMPORTANT TO DO ALL THIS STUFF?

Well, first of all, if you want to get into Heaven, I would recommend doing as much as you can to ensure that will happen, since there are no guarantees. Remember, we are simply proving our case to God on why we are worthy to enter Heaven every single day we live our lives here on earth. What's sad is there are A LOT of people out there in this world who THINK they are going to be getting into Heaven just because they were "good people." For example, they worked for what they got in life; let's say they went to church every week and made a modest donation to the church or charity, took care of their families, and every once in a while would help a person in need. Is this enough to get you into Heaven? According to the Bible, the answer is NO, as you can see in the scriptures and passages that I have put into this book. Just because you go to church and say you believe in God, Jesus, and the Holy Spirit does not mean you are getting into Heaven. Look at the verse in Matthew 7:22-23; even though they drove out demons and performed miracles, that did not matter. The Bible says what you need to do, and I truly hope this book has helped you in your quest to become closer to God, Jesus, and the Holy Spirit. I truly hope that this has helped inspire you to become a true and full believer of God and His unconditional love that He has for every single one of us. My personal testimony by itself should be enough to prove that God is real. He continues to make miracles happen in my life daily!

Just a piece of advice: I have personally found that being a member of several Bible study groups that meet weekly and monthly help keep me grounded and connected to the WORD OF GOD (aka, the Bible, which I also refer to as the Handbook of Life). We pick a chapter and process it together and discuss how it relates to our lives here on earth. I have the same feeling as I would going to a psychologist and unloading all of my feelings on their couch with them for an hour as I have when I leave Bible groups. The only difference is, instead of feeling exhausted and beat down, I am instead inspired, excited, and pretty much fired up ready to go. I just wanted to put this in here about being part of a Bible group because there is just so much good that comes out of it. As a man, we typically only do men-only Bible groups, and women typically do their own women-only Bible groups (I don't know why, to be honest, but it is just the way it is, it seems). Another benefit is I get to spend some QUALITY time around some

NOW, WHY IS IT IMPORTANT TO DO ALL THIS STUFF?

really super awesome God-fearing people who have the same values and belief systems and character that I do. We are all like brothers in this war together. And remember, you are the company you keep. If you are having trouble finding a group, start with your church and ask if they have any small groups that get together to discuss the scripture. I think you will be surprised by the reaction you get; I know I sure was!

So, one reason for writing this book was to bring as many people to Christ and God as I could. The other reason is to grow the overall number of people who walk with Christ. You see, in this world that we live in, evil rules everything, and there is a very good reason for that. You see, the devil himself used to be an angel in Heaven, but he challenged God and LOST, so he was cast down here to earth and told to do whatever he wants UNTIL Jesus comes back! So that is exactly what the devil has done; he has distracted everyone so much with so much "busyness" that most people don't even pay attention to God or Jesus at all. They are too busy living in their smart phones trying to be better than the guy next to them, buying the more expensive car and the more expensive home, all to flaunt what they have for their own egos and pride and personal agendas. That is exactly what the devil wants: people to be infatuated in greed, lust, fornication, envy, jealousness, vanity, fame, success, wealth—ANYTHING BUT GOD! The devil is very real and "prowls around like a roaring lion looking for someone to devour" (1 Peter 5:8). And when you are getting ready to start your journey with Jesus, get ready for some serious spiritual attacks that will inevitably happen to you. Do not be afraid, as you have God on your side, but the devil will try to tempt you and deceive you. Remember, the devil doesn't care about the people who do not believe in God, because he knows he is already going to get them when they go to hell. He is, however, extremely concerned with those who seek God, especially in the beginning part of their journeys because he doesn't want to see them be saved.

There are also very real demons and dark spiritual forces that are here on this earth with us. None that we can see, of course, but oh, they are here, and I have so many other personal stories I could talk about that I experienced during my inpatient psychiatric ward visits. Most people don't know they have a demon feeding on them when they do. The Bible tells us that Satan and his demons can inflict harm on earth by: possessing people to cause them physical and spiritual harm (Matthew 12:22; Mark 5:1-20) and to make them do evil (Luke 22: 3-4), blinding the minds of unbelievers so that they cannot see the light of the Gospel (2 Corinthians 4:4). What are some things that may open yourself up to getting possessed by a demon or demons? Watching movies or television programming that has dark themes/things in them. Listening to music that is demonic in the lyrics and/or messages. Playing with things like

NOW, WHY IS IT IMPORTANT TO DO ALL THIS STUFF?

Ouija boards, contacting psychics for tarot card readings, connecting with mediums, etc.. How about also changing your consciousness? How do you do that: through the use of drugs and alcohol, of course. A lot of liquor stores have "Beer, wine, and SPIRITS" on their signs. And people typically know to stay away from things like hard drugs, but now that marijuana is starting to be legalized for recreational usage in several states throughout the country, I think it is important to talk about that as well. If you read my story, marijuana completely messed with my mind because it let the devil in. The devil was the one who was whispering in my ear that my wife wanted to hire a hit man to kill me. It wasn't the drug; it was the drug that gave the devil access to me because of my consciousness. This is why I now refer to marijuana as the "devil's lettuce." And if my story wasn't enough for you about marijuana, just go to Google and type in marijuana psychosis event or marijuana linked to schizophrenia. There is a lot more to the "weed" of the 21st century that's 30%+ in strength than most people realize, especially parents of teenagers.

Now, it's not all doom and gloom, as there is also some very good news out there too. There are also very good and very real spiritual forces here on this earth as well; think of them as the Divine. People who walk with God and who are "Chosen Ones" with God are Divinely protected. In fact, people who walk with God and trust in Him and believe in Him and have 100% faith in Him are Divinely protected as well. It even says this in the Bible (so you know I'm not making it up). Psalm 23:4 says, "Even though I walk through the darkest valley, I will fear no evil, for you are with me; your rod and your staff, they comfort me." And Isaiah 54:17 says, "No weapon formed against you shall prosper..." Bottom line is this: When you have God, NOTHING can harm you, and you literally have nothing to fear. No matter what the devil brings at you or how he comes to you in your life to challenge you, know that you have God, and God has ALREADY WON the fight against the devil, and He will win it again when the time is right. You can literally just LAUGH in the devil's face (I do)!

God's other message to me writing this book is something much more powerful. Suppose that we could get even half of the people in this country to read this book and even just half of them decided they wanted to give their lives up to God and fully surrender to His will and start walking and living with Jesus every day. That would be 25% of the people in this country, a huge number. That would be a lot of lights out there shining through the darkness. That's how you start exposing the darkness and eradicating it completely. That is how you get rid of all of the evil in this nation and in this world and start cleaning house. You see, I think if we all seek God and surrender to His will and trust in Him and believe in Him and have faith in Him, He will help us change this world for the better. God wants there to be a true Heaven on earth, but He needs

NOW, WHY IS IT IMPORTANT TO DO ALL THIS STUFF?

ALL of **OUR** help to achieve that goal. He needs each and every one of us, young and old, to join together and to surrender our lives to Him so He can show us all how to truly live the lives of our dreams, the lives we are actually called to live by God!

Remember, to do all of this costs ABSOLUTELY NOTHING! This can be done in the comfort of your very own home, on your own time, whenever you are free. Just a few small changes to your life can allow God to transform your life in ways you never thought were possible. He is a miracle worker and is capable of making anything happen. God will change everything for you, BUT YOU HAVE TO ASK HIM TO HELP YOU! That is the key; you need to INVITE Him into your life!

Since God loves to communicate with me through music, I thought these two song choices were appropriate song choices to use to end this book, as one kept popping into my reels page feed last night over and over again and one just hit me today as I was finishing the book up. The first song is Hoobastank's "The Reason," which discusses the "reason" to change who you used to be and to start your life over new. The second song is Skillet's "The Resistance," which discusses the real Spiritual War going on right now between Good and evil on this planet and how we can all RISE UP TOGETHER to defeat evil. Since I cannot publish lyrics here without facing copyright lawsuits, I would highly encourage you to go to Google and watch them both on YouTube to truly feel the full effect of the lyrics...

And I also just started listening to some Christian music that has really started to take hold on me. Check out these artists once you get into the Word with Jesus: Megan Woods, Brandon Lake, Cee Cee Winans, Chuckey Ellis, Matthew West (especially "Unashamed"; I did a podcast about that song on YouTube), and Matt Cooper.

And to completely close out the book, I thought it would be a good idea to insert a prayer that you could read to yourself, so here it goes:

Heavenly Father, I come to You in the Name of Jesus. Your Word says, "whoever shall call on the name of the Lord shall be saved" (Acts 2:21). I am calling on You. I pray and ask Jesus to come into my heart and to be Lord over my life according to Romans 10: 9-10: "For if you confess with your mouth that Jesus is Lord and believe in your heart that God raised him from the dead, you will be saved. For one believes with the heart and so is justified, and one confesses with the mouth and so is saved."

NOW, WHY IS IT IMPORTANT TO DO ALL THIS STUFF?

THANK YOU FOR READING MY BOOK!
DON'T FORGET TO CHECK OUT MY
PODCAST ON YOUTUBE "Is Jesus Real?"
AND CONNECT ON SOCIAL MEDIA
(Facebook – "Michael David Klijanowicz"
and LinkedIn and Mike's Ministries on Facebook)!